FAVOURITE COUNTRY RECIPES

from England's Village Homes

with illustrations by
G. F. Nicholls

SALMON

Index

Cover pictures: *front:* Harvest Time *back:* The Village Green
title page: The Village Cross

Printed and Published by J. Salmon Ltd., Sevenoaks, England ©

Asparagus with Chicken

A delicious way of using up cooked chicken in an asparagus sauce.

1 tin asparagus spears, approx. 10 oz	3 oz butter
¼ pint single cream	1 lb cooked chicken meat
2 hard boiled eggs	1 pint chicken stock
3 oz flour	Lemon juice
	Salt and black pepper

In a saucepan, gently heat the asparagus in the liquor from the tin. Drain the liquor from the asparagus and make up to 1¼ pints with the stock. Melt the butter in a pan, add the flour and cook for one minute. Add the stock gradually, stirring constantly. Add the cream, season and add the lemon juice to taste. Setting aside a few asparagus spears for decoration, chop the rest with the chicken meat, add one chopped hard boiled egg and stir into the sauce; warm through but do not boil. Put the mixture into a hot shallow dish. Arrange the remaining asparagus spears radiating from the centre of the dish with slices of hard boiled egg in between. Serve with triangles of crisply fried bread for tea, or with creamed potatoes and vegetables as a main dish. Serves 4.

Bourton on the Water

Braised Beef

A pot roast cooked with brown ale and beef stock.

2½ lb topside of beef	1 tablespoon tomato purée
2 tablespoons dripping	A bouquet garni
¼ pint brown ale	Sliced mixed vegetables; enough
¼ pint brown stock	to cover the base of a casserole

Set oven to 325°F or Mark 3. Heat the dripping in a pan, add the joint and brown all over; remove and set aside. Put the mixed vegetables in the pan, cover and sauté for five minutes then place in the base of a deep casserole dish. Season well. Place the meat on top of the vegetables. Add the tomato purée, the *bouquet garni* and the ale to the stock and pour over the meat. Season again, then cover tightly and cook for 2-2½ hours. Add more stock if necessary. Remove the *bouquet garni* and serve on a hot dish surrounded by the vegetables. Reduce the liquid to make the gravy; thicken with a little cornflour if desired. Serves 6.

Fish Hotpot

White fish layered in a casserole, with potatoes and mushrooms
with a cheese sauce.

1 lb cod (or any white fish of
  your choice) skinned and cut
  into 1 inch pieces
Seasoned flour
1½ lb boiled potatoes
1 tablespoon lemon juice
4 oz mushrooms, sliced

1 medium sized onion,
  finely chopped
¼ pint white sauce
4 oz grated cheese
Salt and pepper
Chopped parsley or chives
  for decoration

Set oven to 400°F or Mark 6. Well grease a deep casserole dish with butter. Toss the fish in seasoned flour. Slice the potatoes thinly; arrange half the potatoes on the base of the dish, then layer with the fish sprinkled with the lemon juice, then the mushrooms, onions and seasoning. Add 2 oz of the grated cheese to the white sauce and pour over the mixture. Top with the rest of the potatoes. Sprinkle with the remainder of the cheese and bake, uncovered, for 40 minutes. Just before serving sprinkle with the chopped parsley or chives. Serves 4.

Crumbly Fruit Pudding

A traditional steamed, fruit pudding lightened with ground rice.

4 oz self-raising flour	**2 oz soft brown sugar**
2 oz ground rice	**2 oz golden syrup**
4 oz shredded suet	**1 egg**
4 oz mixed dried fruit	**6 tablespoons milk**

Sieve the flour into a mixing bowl and add all the dry ingredients. In a separate bowl beat together the golden syrup and the egg and then add the milk and stir. Add the syrup mixture to the dry ingredients and mix to a soft, dropping consistency. Turn the mixture into a greased 1½ pint pudding basin, cover with greaseproof paper and seal with kitchen foil. Steam for 3-3½ hours, topping up with water as necessary, turn out and serve hot, with custard. Serves 4-6.

Market Day Stew

A lamb casserole; a complete meal with vegetables included.

2 tablespoons cooking oil
1 oz butter
1½ lb boneless leg of lamb,
   cut into 1 inch cubes
2 medium onions peeled and diced
3 carrots, cut into 2 inch sticks
2 sticks celery, trimmed and cut
   into 1 inch slices
1 small turnip, peeled and cut
   into quarters

2 tablespoons flour
1½ pints lamb stock
½ teaspoon dried mixed herbs
Salt and pepper
DUMPLINGS
4 oz self-raising flour
2 oz shredded suet
½ teaspoon dried ground
   rosemary
Cold water to mix

Heat the oil in a frying pan, add the butter and brown the meat, a little at a time and transfer it to a large saucepan. Add the onions, carrots, celery and turnips to the remaining oil and cook gently until the onions are soft. Stir in the flour and cook for a few minutes then add the stock, herbs and salt and pepper. Pour the stock mixture over the meat, cover and simmer for about 1-1½ hours. Meanwhile prepare the dumplings by mixing together the flour, suet, herbs, salt and pepper and adding enough cold water to make a soft dough. Shape into 10 small balls and add to the stew and cook for a further 20 minutes until the dumplings are risen and the meat is tender. Serves 4-6.

Leek Soup

A delicious white soup which can be served hot or cold.

2 pints chicken stock	**1 lb potatoes, cubed**
1 lb leeks, cut into thin rings	**Salt and pepper**
2 oz butter	**Pinch of nutmeg**
2 oz flour	**Pinch of thyme**
2 onions, thinly sliced	**3 tablespoons single cream**

Croutons to garnish

Melt the butter in a pan, add the vegetables and cook for a few minutes without browning. Transfer to a saucepan, add the flour and gradually stir in the stock. Add the nutmeg, thyme and seasoning. Simmer gently for about 40 minutes. Purée in an electric blender. Place in a clean pan and heat through. Just before serving stir in the cream and garnish with croutons. This soup may be served hot or chilled. Serves 6.

Cheese and Potato Bake

A dish comprised of layered cheese and potatoes; a useful supper dish.

2-4 oz butter
6 medium potatoes, peeled
 and cut into thin slices
2 medium onions, peeled
 and thinly sliced
2 cloves garlic, peeled and
 crushed
4 oz Cheddar cheese, grated
1 pint full cream milk
Salt and pepper

Set oven to 325°F or Mark 3. Butter a large, shallow ovenproof dish and arrange a layer of sliced potatoes over the base. Dot with butter, sprinkle with salt and black pepper and add a little crushed garlic with about one quarter of the cheese. Continue making layers like this, finishing with a layer of potatoes topped with cheese. Pour on the milk and cover the dish with kitchen foil. Cook for 1¼ hours, remove the foil and continue cooking for a further 30 minutes until the potatoes are tender. This is an excellent accompaniment to many meat dishes, but also makes a light supper dish served on its own.

Honey Gingerbread

A traditional, dark gingerbread, with the addition of honey and cinnamon.

4 oz butter	**1 teaspoon ground ginger**
4 oz sugar	**½ teaspoon salt**
1 egg, beaten	**6 tablespoons black treacle**
10 oz flour	**6 tablespoons clear honey**
1 teaspoon bicarbonate	**8 fl oz hot water**
of soda	**1 teaspoon cinnamon**

Set oven to 350°F or Mark 4. Grease and line a shallow 9 inch x 9 inch baking tin. Melt the butter in a pan and allow to cool. Beat together the sugar and egg and add to the butter. Combine together the flour, bicarbonate of soda, salt and spices. In a separate bowl mix together the treacle, honey and water. Add the dry and the liquid ingredients alternately to the butter mixture, blending well after each addition. Put into the tin and bake for one hour. Leave to cool for 10 minutes then turn out on to a wire rack.

Bacon and Egg Flan

A family high tea or supper dish.

6 oz shortcrust pastry	**1 heaped tablespoon flour**
1 small onion, grated	**2 eggs, beaten**
½ lb chopped bacon, de-rinded	**½ cup milk**
4 oz Cheddar cheese, grated	**Salt and pepper**

Parsley to garnish

Set oven to 350°F or Mark 4. Roll out the pastry on a floured surface and use to line an 8 inch flan ring. Sprinkle the grated onion and the chopped bacon evenly over the pastry. Mix together the grated cheese and the flour. Stir in the beaten eggs and ½ cup of milk and season with salt and pepper. Pour this mixture over the onion and bacon. Bake for 30 minutes. Decorate with parsley. Serve warm or cold with a green salad. Serves 4.

Lamb with Onions

A dish of thin strips of lamb cooked in soy sauce and sherry,
with broccoli spears.

1 lb lean lamb (from
  shoulder or leg)
1 clove garlic, crushed
4 onions, thinly sliced
1 tablespoon soy sauce
1 tablespoon dry sherry

¼-½ pint chicken stock
1 tablespoon cornflour
Salt and pepper
Pinch of rosemary, chopped
2 tablespoons cooking oil
1 lb cooked broccoli spears

Cut the lamb into thin strips. Heat the oil in a frying pan and fry the meat until it changes colour. Add the very thinly sliced onions. Mix together the garlic, soy sauce, sherry, seasoning and cornflour with the rosemary and the stock. Add to the pan and bring to the boil, stirring all the time; add more stock if the mixture is too thick. Simmer for 2 minutes. Place the mixture in the centre of heated deep serving dish and arrange a circle of broccoli spears around the edge. Serve with rice or baby new potatoes, garnished with chopped mint. Serves 4.

Beef in Pastry

Beef baked in a pastry parcel; an ideal dinner party dish.

2 lb fillet of beef	2 oz butter
8 oz puff pastry	1 dessertspoon mixed herbs
4 oz button mushrooms,	Small tin paté (optional)
thinly sliced	Beaten egg to glaze

Watercress to garnish

Set oven to 425°F or Mark 7. Trim and tie up the fillet. Heat the butter in a pan, add the meat and brown all over, quickly. Transfer to a tin and roast in the oven for 10 minutes. Let the meat cool and remove the string. Meanwhile fry the mushrooms in the butter, add the herbs and leave to cool. Roll out the pastry on a floured surface into a rectangle about ⅛ inch thick. Divide into two pieces, one twice the size of the other. Put the mushrooms in the centre of the larger piece, lay the beef on top of the mushrooms and spread the paté (if desired) on top of the beef. Glaze the edges of the pastry with the beaten egg and wrap up like a parcel. Lay the other piece of pastry on top and press down well. Brush with egg to glaze; decorate with pastry leaves. Place in the oven on a dampened baking sheet. Turn down oven to 400°F or Mark 6 and bake for 45 minutes. Cover with foil if the pastry browns too quickly. Serve garnished with watercress. Serves 6.

Country Paté

A smooth, liver paste with brandy which makes a richly flavoured starter or snack.

¼ lb streaky bacon rashers, rind removed
1½ lb pig's liver
½ lb chicken livers
1 egg, beaten

1 clove of garlic, skinned and crushed
2 tablespoons double cream
2 teaspoons brandy
Salt and black pepper

Set oven to 325°F or Mark 3. Flatten and stretch the bacon rashers with a knife and use them to line a 2 lb loaf tin. Mince the livers together and add the garlic, beaten egg, cream, brandy and seasoning. Mix well. Place the mixture in the tin and cover with kitchen foil. Stand the loaf tin in a tin or dish containing cold water, place in the oven and cook for 2 hours. Allow to cool then cover with a plate and weight down. Leave in the refrigerator overnight. Turn out and serve with a green salad or thin triangular slices of toast.

Oxtail Soup with Rice and Barley

A rich meaty soup, almost a meal in itself.

1 lb oxtail	2 pints beef stock
2 onions	8 peppercorns
2 sticks of celery	2 cloves
2 oz butter	1 medium carrot, grated
2 oz lean ham or bacon, cut into cubes	1 tablespoon rice
	2 tablespoons barley
1 bay leaf	A small glass of sherry
A bouquet garni	1 tablespoon cornflour

Roll the oxtail pieces in seasoned flour and fry in a large saucepan, with the butter. Cut the onions and celery into small pieces and add to the pan with the ham or bacon and fry all together until nicely browned. Add the stock and herbs, peppercorns and cloves; bring to the boil and simmer very gently for 4 hours. Strain and leave to get quite cold, preferably overnight. When cold, take off the fat. Discard the bones, cut up the lean meat of the oxtail into very small pieces and reserve. Put the strained soup into a saucepan and add the grated carrot, the rice and the barley and simmer for 1 hour until the barley is well cooked. Mix the cornflour with the sherry, add to the soup and bring to the boil. Add the oxtail meat last of all, season to taste and continue cooking to re-heat the oxtail. Serve hot.

Braised Liver and Onions

A tasty liver and bacon casserole dish.

About 1 lb lamb's liver, sliced (allow 2 slices per person)
¾ lb onions, thinly sliced
3 leeks, thinly sliced
3 carrots, thinly sliced
1 pint brown stock
Pinch of thyme or sage
2 rashers green bacon, diced

Grated rind and juice of one small orange
1 tablespoon flour
Pinch of nutmeg
1 small teaspoon gravy browning
Salt and pepper
2 oz cooking oil or butter
Cornflour to thicken, if necessary

Set oven to 325°F or Mark 3. Mix the flour, seasoning and nutmeg on a plate and use to coat both sides of the liver. Sauté the liver gently in the oil or butter in a frying pan for a few minutes then remove to a warm plate. Sauté the vegetables in the pan for 5 minutes. Place the vegetables in the base of a casserole dish, cover with the liver and sprinkle the diced bacon over the top. Season well and sprinkle on the grated rind of the orange and the thyme. Place the remaining seasoned flour in the frying pan juices and mix well. Gradually add the stock, the gravy browning and the orange juice. Bring to the boil, stirring constantly. Pour into the casserole. Cover and bake for 30-45 minutes, thickening with cornflour if necessary. Serves 4.

Sand Cake

A traditional British tea-time cake, also popular with a glass of sherry.

2 oz butter	**2 eggs, beaten**
4 oz caster sugar	**2 teaspoons fresh lemon**
1 oz flour	**juice**
4 oz cornflour	**Pinch of salt**
1 level teaspoon baking powder	**Pinch of grated nutmeg**

Set oven to 350°F or Mark 4. Grease and line a 2 inch deep, 7 inch round cake tin. Mix the butter and sugar well together in a bowl, add the beaten eggs and beat well. Fold in the sieved flours, the salt and the nutmeg. Lastly add the lemon juice and mix well. Place in the tin and level off the top. Bake for about 30 minutes until firm and golden. Leave in the tin for 15 minutes then turn out on to a wire rack. Dredge the top with a little sieved icing sugar.

Cheese Pudding

A light, baked pudding of breadcrumbs, eggs and grated cheese.

2 eggs, beaten
1 small onion, finely
  chopped
Salt and black pepper
Dash of Worcestershire sauce
1 teaspoon made mustard
6 oz strong grated cheese

3 tomatoes, sliced
1 cup fresh breadcrumbs,
  brown or white
1 oz butter
¾ pint milk
Chopped chives or parsley
  for decoration

Set oven to 350°F or Mark 4. Grease a casserole dish with butter. Mix the breadcrumbs, onions, salt, pepper and 4 oz of the cheese in the casserole. Pour the milk on to the beaten eggs, add the Worcestershire sauce and mustard and mix together. Pour over the breadcrumb mixture. Sprinkle the rest of the cheese on top. Cover with the sliced tomatoes. Sprinkle with black pepper and dot with butter. Bake for about one hour until firm and golden. Decorate with chopped chives or parsley. Serve with watercress or endive and crusty wholemeal rolls. Serves 4.

Steak and Kidney Pudding

One of the all-time greats of English cooking.

4 oz shredded suet	**1½ lb bladebone steak**
8 oz self raising flour	**¼ lb ox kidney**
Salt and black pepper	**¼ lb mushrooms**
¼ pint cold water	**1 dozen oysters (optional)**

Mix together in a bowl the flour and suet with the seasoning. Add water and mix together to form a soft dough. Cut the meat into small pieces, discarding any gristle or fat. Cut up the kidney after taking out the white core. Cut up the mushrooms. Toss all in seasoned flour. Grease a 1½-2 pint pudding basin. Roll out the suet pastry on a floured surface. Line the basin with two thirds of the paste, reserving one third for the lid. Put the meat, kidney, mushrooms and oysters (if desired) in layers in the basin, sprinkling a little flour with each layer. When the basin is full, add cold water nearly to the brim. Put on a pastry lid, moistening round the edge and pressing down well to make a good seal. Cover the top with greased greaseproof paper and tie a cloth over it, or use kitchen foil. Put the pudding in a saucepan of boiling water, not more than halfway up the basin. Simmer for three hours, topping up the water as necessary. Brown ale can be substituted for water in the pudding; it improves the taste of the gravy. Serves 4-6.

Mixed Sweet Pickle

Crunchy vegetables pickled in sweetened white vinegar.

2 lbs cucumber	**6 oz sugar**
1 lb onions, peeled	**2 teaspoons mustard seed**
½ lb cauliflower curd	**3 cloves**
2 oz salt	**1 teaspoon ground ginger**
1 pint white vinegar	**1 teaspoon turmeric**

Dice the cucumber and onions into very small pieces and break up the cauliflower curds into small florets. Place all the vegetables into a pottery dish, sprinkle with the salt and leave for 3 hours. Drain and rinse thoroughly. Put the vegetables with the vinegar, sugar and the spices into a stainless steel or enamel saucepan (not aluminium) and heat gently, bringing to the boil. Remove from the heat, pack into hot jars and seal with vinegar-proof lids. Leave for 6-8 weeks to mature.

Mince Pies

One of the traditional accompaniments to Christmas.

1 lb cooking apples
A 'walnut' of butter
1 lb mixed dried fruit
2 oz blanched almonds, chopped
8 oz soft brown sugar
2 oz shredded suet

½ level teaspoon grated nutmeg
½ level teaspoon ground cinnamon
Sherry (optional)
The juice of one small orange
  and one lemon
Shortcrust pastry

Peel, core and chop the apples and cook in a little butter with the saucepan lid on, so as not to brown or burn them. Allow to cool. Add the other ingredients and mix well together with the juice of the orange and lemon. Add some sherry (if desired) if the mixture appears too dry, otherwise add a little more orange juice. Grease some patty tins. Roll out thinly the shortcrust pastry on a lightly floured surface and use to line the patty tins. Put a generous spoonful of the mincemeat into each pie. Cut suitable size lids, moisten the edges and put on firmly. Prick with a fork. Bake in a hot oven, 400°F or Mark 6, for approximately 10-15 minutes until golden brown.

Nut and Apple Cake

This coffee and nut sponge cake has an apple and apricot jam filling.

4 oz butter	4 oz caster sugar
2 eggs, separated	1½ oz roasted ground hazelnuts
4 oz self-raising flour	1 tablespoon warm milk
Pinch of salt	1 teaspoon instant coffee

FILLING

Rind and juice of ½ lemon	2 tablespoons apricot jam
1 lb Cox's Orange Pippin apples	2 oz melted plain chocolate or sifted icing sugar for topping

Set oven to 375°F or Mark 5. Grease and line a 8 inch round cake tin. Soften the butter in a bowl, add the sugar and beat until fluffy. Add the egg yolks, nuts, sifted flour and salt. Dissolve the coffee in the milk and add to the mixture; then fold in the stiffly beaten egg whites. Turn into the prepared tin and bake for about 25 minutes until firm to the touch. Turn on to a wire rack and leave to cool. Meanwhile peel, core and slice the apples and place in a pan with the jam and the rind and juice of ½ lemon. Cover and cook gently until soft. Cool. Split the cake in half and fill with the apple mixture. For the top of the cake, either spread with 2 oz of melted plain chocolate or sprinkle with sifted icing sugar.

Carrot Soup

A rich, thick and satisfying vegetable soup.

1 lb carrots, chopped
2 sticks celery, chopped
1 small onion, finely chopped
4 oz turnips, cubed
1 rasher bacon, chopped
1½ pints chicken stock
1 oz butter

A bouquet garni
Pinch of freshly grated
  nutmeg
2 oz flour
¼ pint milk
2 tablespoons single cream
Chopped parsley

Melt the butter in a pan and fry the bacon and vegetables for a few minutes. Transfer to a saucepan, add the stock and the *bouquet garni* (tied to the pan handle for easy removal later) and season well. Cover and simmer gently for about 45 minutes. Remove the *bouquet garni* and then purée the mixture in an electric blender for a few seconds. Place in a clean pan and re-heat. Add the nutmeg. Blend the flour and milk to a smooth cream and gradually add to the pan, stirring until it thickens. Check the seasoning. Just before serving, stir in the cream and sprinkle the top with parsley. Serves 6.

Tomato and Cheese Tart

A savoury, vegetarian flan; a light luncheon or supper dish.

6 oz shortcrust pastry
FILLING

4½ oz fresh white breadcrumbs
8 tomatoes, sliced
Salt and pepper
6 oz. grated cheese (Cheddar or Gruyere)

1 tablespoon chopped mixed herbs and parsley
Grated nutmeg (optional)
1 dessertspoon anchovy essence
¼ pint double cream

Set oven to 400°F or Mark 6. Roll out the pastry on a floured surface and use to line an 8 inch flan ring. Lightly brown the breadcrumbs on a tray in the oven, then place them in the bottom of the flan case. Arrange the sliced tomatoes over the breadcrumbs and season. Mix together the cheese, cream, herbs and anchovy essence with a sprinkling of black pepper. Add a little grated nutmeg (if desired). Spoon the mixture over the tomatoes and bake for 30-40 minutes. After 20 minutes lower the oven temperature to 350°F or Mark 4. Serve warm or cold with a green salad. Serves 4.

Haddock Charlotte

A simple and easily prepared supper dish.

1 lb smoked or fresh haddock
  minced or chopped
1 egg, beaten
5 fl oz milk
Grated rind of ½ lemon

1 tablespoon chopped fresh parsley
Salt and pepper
5 slices white bread, buttered,
  with crusts removed and cut
  into fingers

Set oven to 350°F or Mark 4. Separate the haddock flesh from the skin and bones and mince or chop into small pieces. Mix together in a bowl the fish, beaten egg, milk, lemon rind and parsley with salt and pepper to taste. Line a pie dish with a layer of bread and butter fingers, butter side outwards. Put a layer of half the fish mixture into the pie dish, cover with a layer of bread and butter, add the remaining fish mixture and finish with a layer of bread and butter, butter side upwards. Bake for 40-45 minutes until the top is crisp and golden brown. Serve with warm crusty bread and butter. Serves 4.

Rich Plum Cake

A celebration cake full of dried fruit and flavoured with rum or brandy.

½ lb butter
½ lb caster sugar
½ lb currants
½ lb candied peel
½ lb almonds, blanched
  and chopped
¼ lb glacé cherries

½ lb flour
½ lb raisins
½ lb sultanas
6 medium eggs, lightly
  beaten
2 tablespoons rum or brandy
1 tablespoon black coffee

Set oven to 325°F or Mark 3. Grease an 8 inch cake tin. Cream together the butter and sugar in a bowl. Add the lightly beaten eggs, one at a time, with a teaspoon of flour after the third egg. Beat thoroughly. Mix all the fruit together with half the flour. Stir the rest of the flour, with the peel and almonds, into the egg and butter mixture. Then add the floured fruit, the rum or brandy and the coffee and mix well. Place in the tin and bake for 2½ hours or longer until a skewer pushed into the cake comes out clean. To prevent the sides from browning, tie a band of brown paper round the outside of the tin. Leave to cool for about 10 minutes and turn out on to a wire rack.

Tripe and Onions

*Economical and digestible, a traditional dish long popular, particularly
in the Northern counties.*

1 lb tripe	**1 pint milk**
1 lb onions	**¼ teaspoon salt**
Black pepper to taste	

Cut the tripe in small strips about 2-inches long. Slice the onions. Put the tripe and
the onions into a stewpan with a tight fitting lid, or into a casserole, together with
the milk and seasoning. Cook slowly for 3 hours until the tripe is thoroughly soft.
Remove the tripe from the liquid on to a warm dish and then thicken the gravy with
a little cornflour. Serve the tripe garnished with chopped parsley and with the
thickened gravy, accompanied by potatoes that have been mashed with a generous
amount of butter. Serves 4.

Celebration Lamb

A lamb and asparagus dish for special occasions.

2 lb leg of lamb, cut into 2 inch pieces	**2 onions, thinly sliced**
Seasoned flour	**½ pint lamb stock**
2 lb asparagus, cooked	**5 fl oz double cream**
2 oz butter	**Pinch of rosemary**
2 oz flour	**Salt and pepper**
	A few drops of fresh lemon juice

Set oven to 325°F or Mark 3. Melt the butter in a frying pan. Coat the meat with seasoned flour and cook, a little at a time, in the butter until browned all over. Place in an ovenproof dish. Add the onions to the pan and cook for a few minutes. Add the stock and when hot pour over the meat and mix well. Add the rosemary, cover and cook in the oven for about 1 hour until the meat is tender. Drain the meat and put on to a warm serving dish. Drain the cooked asparagus, cut off the tips and arrange them around the meat. Place the stems of the asparagus with 2 tablespoons of liquid from the casserole in a liquidizer and, when blended, add to the casserole together with the cream, lemon juice and seasoning. Re-heat on the stove, stirring all the time and then pour over meat. Serve with baby potatoes and buttered carrots. Serves 4-6.

Queen Cakes

Versatile small, light cakes with a variety of alternative flavourings.

4 oz self-raising flour	**1 egg**
2 oz soft margarine	**2 to 3 tablespoons milk**
2 oz caster sugar	**½ to 1 teaspoon vanilla essence**

Set oven to 375°F or Mark 5. Cream the margarine and sugar together in a bowl until light and fluffy. Beat the egg with a small quantity of the milk and add the vanilla essence. Gradually stir in the egg mixture alternately with the flour (and any alternative flavourings as appropriate) into the fat/sugar mixture, adding the rest of milk if necessary. The mixture should be thick but loose enough to drop easily from a spoon. Put a heaped teaspoon of the mixture into greased bun tins, or paper bun cases on a baking tray and bake towards the top of the oven for 20 minutes. Turn out on to a wire rack.

Variations: alternative flavours can be substituted for the vanilla essence as follows: ½ oz. grated chocolate with ½ oz. dessicated coconut: 1½-2 oz. chopped glacé cherries: 1½-2 oz chopped crystallised ginger: 1½-2 oz chopped dates: 1 oz chopped mixed peel with ½-1 oz chopped nuts.

Pork in Cream Sauce

A pork and mushroom hotpot with paprika, mushrooms and sherry.

2-3 pork fillets	1 level dessertspoon flour
1 oz butter	1 level dessertspoon paprika pepper
2 shallots	3 oz button mushrooms
1 wineglass sherry	Salt and pepper
¼ pint chicken stock	3 fl oz single cream

Chop the shallots. Cut the pork fillets into bite-size pieces. Melt the butter in a frying pan and fry the pork pieces quickly on both sides to seal. Add the shallots and paprika, lower the heat and cook for 3 minutes. Stir in the flour, sherry, seasoning and stock and simmer gently for 30 minutes. Add the mushrooms and simmer for a further 2 minutes. Add the cream. Put into a hot serving dish and serve with rice or creamed potatoes and a green vegetable. Serves 4.

Onion and Raisin Hotpot

*An unusual dish, to be served hot with cheesey baked potatoes
or cold with cold meat.*

20 small even-sized onions **6 oz seedless raisins**
3 tablespoons vegetable oil **½ pint white wine**
4 oz small button mushrooms **Pinch of dried thyme**
½ pint tomato purée **1 teaspoon sugar**
Salt and black pepper

Peel the onions and cook in boiling salted water for 5 minutes. Drain and toss in heated oil in a frying pan until pale golden in colour. Add the mushrooms and cook for 2 minutes. Add the raisins, wine, thyme, tomato purée, sugar and seasoning to the pan. Cover and cook very gently for 20 minutes; uncover and cook for 10 minutes longer to allow some of the liquid to evaporate. Serve hot with baked potatoes topped with cheese browned under the grill; or cold with cold sliced meats and crusty bread. Serves 4.

Stuffed Marrow

Baked marrow stuffed with a cheese, egg and white wine filling;
a vegetarian dish.

2 small young marrows	**2 tablespoons single cream**
Salt and pepper	**¼ pint white wine**
2 tablespoons mixed herbs (chives,	**4 oz strong hard cheese, grated**
parsley, dill, lemon thyme)	**2 hard boiled eggs, chopped**
2 oz butter	**3-4 oz fresh breadcrumbs**

Set oven to 350°F or Mark 4. Cut the marrows in half, lengthwise and remove the centre pith and the pips. Butter a large rectangular ovenproof dish, large enough to take the 4 pieces of marrow side by side. Boil the marrows in a pan of salted water for 10 minutes, then drain well and place, cut sides up, in the dish. Season well. Combine the breadcrumbs, cheese, hard boiled eggs, cream and herbs together and press the mixture into the marrow halves. Dot with butter and season again. Pour the wine into the base of the dish, cover with foil and bake for 30-40 minutes until the marrow is completely tender. Serves 4.

Orange and Walnut Cake

A plain cake flavoured with orange juice and marmalade.

6 oz butter, softened
Grated rind of an orange
6 oz caster sugar
2 eggs, separated
10 oz flour
1 teaspoon baking powder
2 oz orange marmalade
3 oz chopped walnuts

5 tablespoons water and
  orange juice, mixed
WATER ICING
Made with sifted icing sugar
  and sufficient water and
  strained orange juice to give
  a light coating consistency
Walnut halves to decorate

Set oven to 350°F or Mark 4. Grease and flour a round 7 inch cake tin and line the base. Cream together in a bowl the butter, orange rind and sugar until light and fluffy, then beat in the egg yolks. Sift the flour and baking powder together and fold in. Add the marmalade, chopped walnuts and the water/orange juice mixture and combine lightly. Whisk the egg whites until they stand in soft peaks and fold into the mixture. Turn into the tin and smooth over lightly. Bake for 1 to 1¼ hours, or until a skewer inserted into the cake comes out clean, covering with foil if it appears to be browning too quickly. Allow to stand in the tin for 5 to 10 minutes, then turn out and cool on a wire rack. When completely cold, lightly brush off the top of the cake and drizzle over it the water icing; decorate with walnut halves.

Apple Pasties

Individual puff pastry apple pies, useful as a cold snack.

2 large cooking apples	**A 'walnut' of butter**
6 oz sugar	**8 oz puff pastry**
3 cloves	**White of egg**

Peel the apples, cut into quarters and core. Cut into small pieces and put into a saucepan with the sugar, cloves and butter. Cook very slowly, with the lid on, so that the apple only only just cooks and does not brown or burn. Then leave to get quite cold. Take out the cloves. Roll out the pastry to ⅛-¼ inch thick on a lightly floured surface and cut out rounds the size of a saucer. Put a tablespoon of the cooked apples on each round of pastry, dampen the edges and fold over in the form of a Cornish pasty. Crimp the edges with the finger and thumb. Brush over with white of egg and sprinkle with sugar. Place on a greased baking sheet and bake in a hot oven, 400°F or Mark 6, until they are golden brown. Remove from the baking sheet and cool on a wire rack.

Chicken and Bacon Casserole

A whole chicken casseroled in red wine with onions, mushrooms and bacon.

4 lb oven-ready fresh chicken	8 oz button mushrooms
2 tablespoons cooking oil	1 clove garlic, crushed
2 oz butter	1 teaspoon mixed herbs
6 oz bacon, de-rinded and cubed	1 bayleaf
12 small onions, peeled	1 pint red table wine

Salt and black pepper

Set oven to 325°F or Mark 3. Heat the butter and oil in a large frying pan and brown the chicken all over. Remove from the pan and place in an ovenproof dish. Fry the bacon, onions, mushrooms and garlic for a few minutes, add the herbs, bayleaf, seasoning and wine and mix well. Pour over the chicken. Cover and cook for 1½-2 hours until the chicken is tender. Place the chicken on a warmed serving dish and keep hot. Remove the bayleaf. Strain the liquid and thicken, if necessary, with a little cornflour and serve as gravy. Serve with boiled potatoes and brussels sprouts arranged around the chicken on the dish. Serves 6.

Fluffy Ginger Sponge

A fat-less sponge, flavoured with ginger and cocoa, sandwiched
with cream and crystallised ginger.

4 oz sugar	2 level teaspoons cream of tartar
2 oz cornflour	1 level teaspoon bicarbonate of soda
2 level tablespoons flour	1 dessertspoon warmed golden syrup
2 level teaspoons ground ginger	4 eggs, separated
2 level teaspoons ground cinnamon	Whipped cream
2 level teaspoons cocoa powder	Crystallised ginger

Set oven to 350°F or Mark 4. Grease and flour two deep 7 inch sandwich tins. Sift the flours and spices, cocoa, bicarbonate of soda and cream of tartar together four times to mix them thoroughly. In a bowl, whisk the egg whites until stiff then gradually add the sugar, whisking well after each addition. Add the egg yolks all at once. Sift the flour mixture on to eggs and sugar mixture and fold in gently. Pour in the warmed syrup and mix in. Pour into the tins and bake for 15-20 minutes until firm. Turn out on to a wire rack. When cool, sandwich together with whipped cream and chopped crystallised ginger. Eat the same day.

METRIC CONVERSIONS

The weights, measures and oven temperatures used in the preceding recipes can be easily converted to their metric equivalents. The conversions listed below are only approximate, having been rounded up or down as may be appropriate.

Weights

Avoirdupois	Metric
1 oz.	just under 30 grams
4 oz. (¼ lb.)	app. 115 grams
8 oz. (½ lb.)	app. 230 grams
1 lb.	454 grams

Liquid Measures

Imperial	Metric
1 tablespoon (liquid only)	20 millilitres
1 fl. oz.	app. 30 millilitres
1 gill (¼ pt.)	app. 145 millilitres
½ pt.	app. 285 millilitres
1 pt.	app. 570 millilitres
1 qt.	app. 1.140 litres

Oven Temperatures

	°Fahrenheit	Gas Mark	°Celsius
Slow	300	2	150
	325	3	170
Moderate	350	4	180
	375	5	190
	400	6	200
Hot	425	7	220
	450	8	230
	475	9	240

Flour as specified in these recipes refers to Plain Flour unless otherwise described.